AmericanGirl Library®

Brain Waves

Puzzle Book

By **Rick Walton**

Illustrated by
Lori Osiecki

Editorial Development: Trula Magruder, Michelle Watkins
Art Direction and Design: Chris David; Illustrations: Lori Osiecki;
Production: Kendra Pulvermacher, Mindy Rappe

Dear Puzzler!

Treat your brain to hours of mind-boggling fun! You'll moan, groan, chuckle, and cheer as you steer your way through crosswords, tricky teasers, silly riddles, and so much more. Can't solve the puzzle? Try the hints along the edge. (Or peek at the answers in back when no one's looking!) But you don't have to solve solo. Challenge a friend to a tricky teaser. Figure out a befuddler with your family. Take *Brain Waves* to the pool, camp, a pal's house, school— anywhere you plan on taking your brain!

Check it out, then check it off!

Art Smarts

- [ ] Hold the Line (page 12)
- [ ] Hold the Line (page 58)
- [ ] Signs of Spring
- [ ] Just Passing Through
- [ ] Count Your Q's ...
- [ ] ...and Cones!

Chew on This!

- [ ] Straight Walking
- [ ] Wheely Fun!
- [ ] A Tad Bad
- [ ] Bounce Back!
- [ ] Trouble
- [ ] Family Tree
- [ ] What's the Matter, Adder?
- [ ] Spooky Stuff?
- [ ] Leg Work
- [ ] Page Count

Compound Fun

- [ ] Compound Fractures (page 22)
- [ ] Compound Fractures (page 93)
- [ ] Twist and Shout
- [ ] Winding Words
- [ ] Extra Serving!

Crosswords & Cross Grids

- [ ] Jewel Jumble
- [ ] Show Time!
- [ ] Stormy Subject
- [ ] "C" You This Weekend!
- [ ] Face the Music
- [ ] Ballet Play

Climb the Ladder

- [ ] Presto Pets!
- [ ] One + One = One
- [ ] Animal Magic (page 40)
- [ ] Animal Magic (page 90)
- [ ] Mixed Messages (page 46)
- [ ] Mixed Messages (page 100)
- [ ] Patriotic Pyramid
- [ ] One + One = ∧Another One
- [ ] O Brother!

Make a Connection

- [ ] Dot-to-Dot
- [ ] What's in a Name?
- [ ] Movie Mix-Up
- [ ] Botched-Up Books (page 45)
- [ ] Botched-Up Books (page 96)
- [ ] Go for the Gold!
- [ ] Castle Crisis
- [ ] Clover to You!
- [ ] Cross Country
- [ ] Grover's Garden
- [ ] Stop, Look, and Be A-mazed!
- [ ] Star Power

Stuck?
Answers start on page 118!

Hi Ya!

Greetings, hello, and welcome to your first word search. The listed words are common greetings from around the world. Find them going up, down, backward, forward, and diagonally.

```
H  B  U  O  N  G  I  O  R  N  O  C
O  I  O  O  B  Y  L  L  O  O  I  D
A  B  Y  N  I  D  S  L  A  W  Y  R
L  S  I  A  J  W  A  E  H  H  A  A
O  G  L  H  R  O  D  H  I  A  D  W
H  N  G  O  E  H  U  A  N  I  D  I
A  I  E  J  H  J  Y  R  R  J  O  H
A  T  A  E  L  A  S  O  X  L  O  C
L  E  P  V  D  M  O  H  U  E  G  I
O  E  C  D  Y  B  A  L  L  A  H  N
H  R  I  O  L  O  S  O  D  W  E  O
O  G  A  T  N  E  T  U  G  O  L  K
```

ALOHA (Hawaiian)	DAG (Afrikaans)	HAI (Chinese)	HOWDY
AHOJ (Czech)	GIDDAY (Australian)	HALLA (Swedish)	JAMBO (Swahili)
BONJOUR (French)	GOOD DAY	HELLO	KONICHIWA (Japanese)
BUON GIORNO (Italian)	GREETINGS	HIYA	NI HAO (Chinese)
	GUTEN TAG (German)	HOLA (Spanish)	

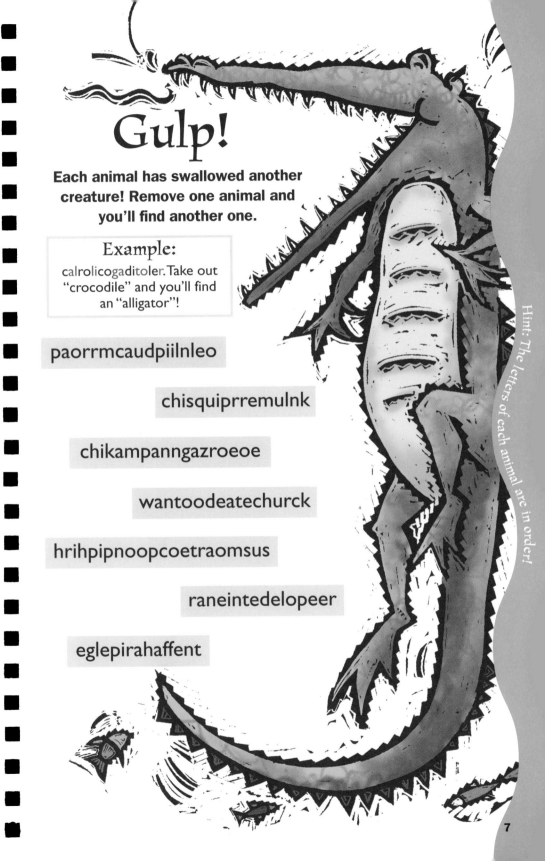

Gulp!

Each animal has swallowed another creature! Remove one animal and you'll find another one.

Example:
calrolicogaditoler. Take out "crocodile" and you'll find an "alligator"!

paorrmcaudpiilnleo

chisquiprremulnk

chikampanngazroeoe

wantoodeatechurck

hrihpipnoopcoetraomsus

raneintedelopeer

eglepirahaffent

Silly Sentences

To find a silly sentence, put the same letter in each blank.

Example:
__ate __nits __itten __ilts.
becomes
Kate Knits Kitten Kilts.

____live ____pens ____scar's ____ranges.

____ice, ____eat ____arrow ____oodles ____ever ____eed ____uts.

____live, ____lice ____muses ____corns ____gain. ____lone, ____be ____pplauds ____rmadillos.

____lack ____ears ____luster. ____old ____eagles ____ark. ____rave, ____rash ____umblebees ____other ____oisterous ____oys.

____our ____lawless ____lying ____airies ____etch
____rail, ____rightful ____allen ____owl.

____andy's ____razed ____at ____raves ____old,
____huggable ____ream.

__anger, ___ear ____ad! ____river ____an
____rags ____inner ____own ____rains!

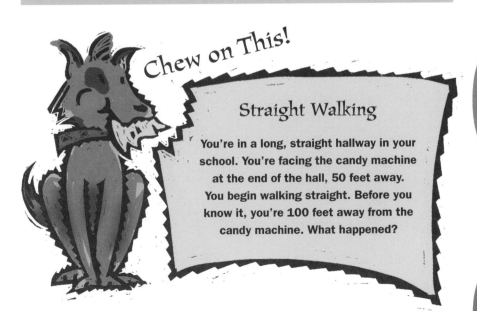

Chew on This!

Straight Walking

You're in a long, straight hallway in your school. You're facing the candy machine at the end of the hall, 50 feet away. You begin walking straight. Before you know it, you're 100 feet away from the candy machine. What happened?

What's the Color?

In each of the lists below, all of the words come from the letters in the name of a color.

> Example:
> lowly, owe, owl, well
> all come from yellow.

1. back, cab, lab, lack

2. lure, pulp, pure, rule

3. born, bow, now, own

4. age, anger, gone, groan

5. live, love, olive, toe

6. cart, castle, race, rats

7. arena, emu, aquarium

8. dare, deal, end, even

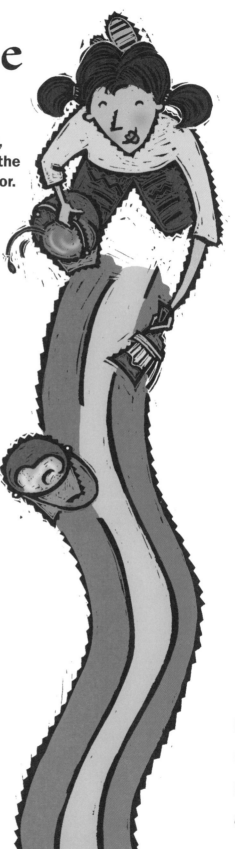

Hint: Make a list that includes more colors than the basic eight. See if any fit.

Presto Pets!

**Did you know that you can turn a dog into a cat?
Just follow the clues to change one letter at a time.**

Example:

d o g

<u>D</u> <u>o</u> <u>t</u>   Nickname for Dorothy

<u>c</u> <u>o</u> <u>t</u>   A cat could sleep on this.

c a t

Can you do it in four steps?

d o g

___ ___ ___ What a pig!

___ ___ ___ Not cold

___ ___ ___ One famous cat wears this.

c a t

In five steps?

d o g

___ ___ ___ Dogs do this to make holes.

___ ___ ___ What a hog!

___ ___ ___ What the dog dug

___ ___ ___ A kind touch on the head

c a t

Hold the Line

Draw these shapes without lifting your pencil from the paper or retracing the lines.

Jewel Jumble

Fit the jewels into the cross grid.

Hint: Start with words that don't have the same number of letters as any other words. Usually these will be the longest words.

Amber	Garnet	Quartz
Amethyst	Jade	Ruby
Beryl	Jasper	Tourmaline
Diamond	Onyx	Turquoise
Emerald	Opal	

Brain Benders

Count on these teasers to cause you confusion.

Hint: Write out the numbers next to the numerals.

It All Adds Up

Yes, these numbers are in order. But there are a couple missing. Can you figure out where 7 and 8 go?

1
2
6
10
4
5
9
3
11
12

What a Funny Way to Count

These numbers are in order, too, but 10 is missing. Can you figure out where 10 should go?

80
50
40
90
70
60
30
20

Dot-to-Dot

Find the path that answers each riddle. You can follow the letters in any direction as long as they're connected by a line. You won't use all the letters in the puzzle.

Hint: All the vowels are used in the answers.

What's black and white and found at the north pole?

B   D   T   M   S

R   E   Z   S   O   D

L   B   R   L   V

C   A   X   A

start

What's found in Australia and comes back at you if you throw it?

S   A   K   K   L

R   R   G   A   F   S

O   N   D   M   W

O   A   K   A

start

15

Safari Search

Fill in the blanks with the name of an animal to make a word. Add that animal to your list on page 17. You should discover six different animals.

1. ACRO**bat**

2. COPY____

3. DANDE_____

4. OVER_____ING

5. ____ARD

6. BIL_____

7. _____APULT

8. KA_____E

9. VA____ION

10. MEDAL_____

11. PI____E

12. ____HROOM

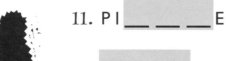

13. C _ _ _ _ E R

14. S C _ _ _ _ C H

15. S _ _ _ _ L

16. M I L _ _ _ _ _

Your list of animals:

_b a t_ _____ _____

_____ _____

_____ _____

Chew on This!

Wheely Fun!

Your family owns two cars, three bicycles, and one tricycle. How many wheels do they have altogether?

Words Worth Eating

How's your appetite for wacky words? The first word is a question. The rest answer that question.

Whatwhatlunchlunchlunchlunchdayday?

_____

left
___
pizza

_____

SOUP

_____

geg gge with s t a c

_____

Sweet Somethings

After lunch, your next question is the wacky word below.
Following it are the answers.

WhatwhatDDDDert?

_____

pi pumpk e

_____

br rays ead

_____

EEEEEEEEE

_____

lem
――――
pie

_____

ban/ana

_____

What's in a Name?

Follow the meandering lines to "C" the meaning of each of these girls' names.

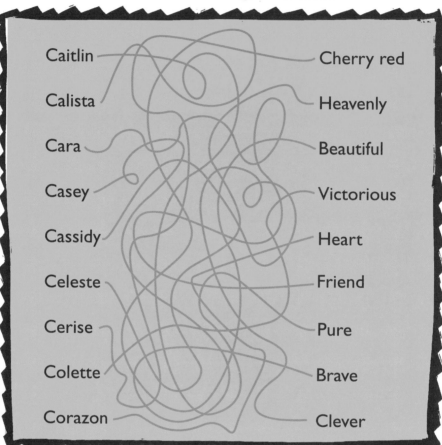

Caitlin   Cherry red

Calista   Heavenly

Cara   Beautiful

Casey   Victorious

Cassidy   Heart

Celeste   Friend

Cerise   Pure

Colette   Brave

Corazon   Clever

 # Fruit Salad

Try your skills at this sweet-and-sour word search.
Listed words go up, down, backward, forward, and diagonally.

APPLE	GOOSEBERRY	LIME	PLUM
APRICOT	GRAPE	MANGO	POMEGRANATE
BANANA	GUAVA	ORANGE	PRUNE
DATE	KIWI	PAPAYA	QUINCE
ELDERBERRY	KUMQUAT	PEACH	TANGERINE
FIG	LEMON	PEAR	

```
U  I  W  I  K  G  C  E  N  U  R  P
P  L  U  M  L  E  M  O  N  P  G  B
H  E  E  T  G  T  T  R  E  I  H  G
C  N  L  A  X  A  R  A  F  L  O  A
A  I  D  U  Y  N  R  N  D  O  N  N
E  R  E  Q  T  A  P  G  S  A  Q  O
P  E  R  M  O  R  P  E  N  P  U  M
A  G  B  U  C  G  B  A  N  P  I  M
V  N  E  K  I  E  B  L  P  L  N  I
A  A  R  W  R  M  L  I  M  E  C  S
U  T  R  R  P  O  G  R  A  P  E  R
G  Y  Y  E  A  P  M  A  N  G  O  E
```

bed _time_
some _time_
spring _time_
summer _time_

bob_____
copy_____
tom_____
wild_____

fly_____
news_____
sand_____
wall_____

Hint: Try to get one in each group, then see if the ending works with the rest of the words.

Compound Fractures

Can you figure out which word turns each of these sets into compound words?

barn_____
court_____
farm_____
grave_____
ship_____

cat_____
gold_____
jelly_____
shell_____
sword_____

bill_____
cup_____
dash_____
key_____
over_____
surf_____

Water Use Haying?

Repeat these sentences to see if you can figure out what was said.

Hint: Put the end of one word with the beginning of the next. What does it sound like?

1. Bee oh Matt's icks Ford inner.

2. Y'ogre and mosk humming toove is it.

3. Itcher tern udu thud ishes.

4. Willy ubay bees it Yorba ruther hands his tour?

5. Getcher ham worked on beef or Yukon pull hay.

6. Goo jobbed ear oog atoll laze!

ABC, 123

Fill in three consecutive letters to complete each word so that it fits the category.

Summer

__ A __ K Y A R __

L __ A P __ R O __

L A U __ __ __ __ N G

T H I __ __ __ __ Y

__ A __ K B E N __ S

__ E __ O __ A D E

Describe It

W O N __ __ __ R __ U L

I N __ R E __ __ I B L __

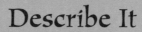

T __ R R I __ __ Y I N __

__ P E C __ A C __ __ L A R

24

Oops!

__ M __ U L A N __ E

B U T T __ R __ I N __ E R S

__ __ __ __ M B L E

A C __ I __ __ __ N T

Chew on This!

A Tad Bad

Thirty furious elephants stomped through the jungle, caught the naughty monkeys, and threw them into a lake. But the monkeys just laughed. Find the mispelled word in this paragraph.

Show Time!

Across

3. Light, fluffy snack food
4. All the actors in a movie
6. When crowds attend a movie, it's a ____!
8. A favorite movie sipper
10. Fast-paced film style
12. Famous actors often are called movie ____.
14. The place between rows of seats
16. The person who oversees the entire movie
18. Another term for "movie"
19. Dolby, THX, or stereo
22. The place you see movies
24. A movie can be shot on location or on a ____.
25. When a shot's over, the director might shout this.
26. The ones who help make a movie but aren't in it
27. Before a premiere, some theaters might show a ____ ____ (2 words).

Down

1. When a great movie is over, you may hear this.
2. Expect to stand in this if the film's a hit.
5. People who pretend to be characters
7. The paper stub you buy
8. This describes the actors' lines and action.
9. Sweet movie treat
11. An ad that shows movie scenes is called a ____.
13. What you see a movie on
15. What you'll hear if a film is funny
17. The part an actor plays
20. Scenes not in the movie, but sometimes shown in credits
21. In action films, most actors have a stunt ____.
23. The person who handles the business dealings for each actor
26. A British word for movie theater

Quiet on the set—until all you movie buffs figure out this Academy Award–winning crossword!

Pick-Up Sticks

Move two of these popsicle sticks
to another location to find
something you can't buy.

Brain Benders

**Figure out these
mind-expanding teasers.**

A Giant Ant and a Miniature Whale
(Oh Yeah, and a Horse)

A giant ant, a regular-sized horse, and a
miniature blue whale went to dinner. The
ant weighed twice as much as the horse.
The horse weighed twice as much as the
whale. All together, they weighed 3,500
pounds. How much did each weigh?

Movie Mix-Up

Films-R-Us sent movies to the Kidz Film Festival, but the double reels got all mixed up. Draw a line from the reel on the left to its match on the right.

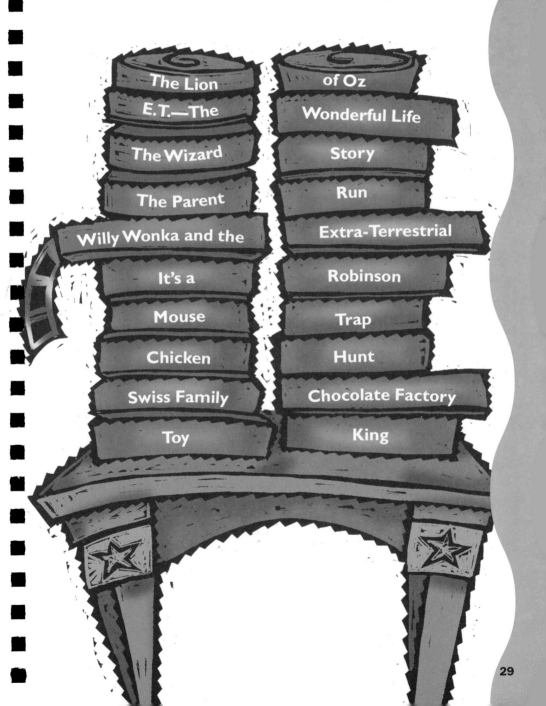

The Lion — of Oz

E.T.—The — Wonderful Life

The Wizard — Story

The Parent — Run

Willy Wonka and the — Extra-Terrestrial

It's a — Robinson

Mouse — Trap

Chicken — Hunt

Swiss Family — Chocolate Factory

Toy — King

Switch Witch

You know the witch who turns the frog into the prince, right? Her sister prefers rhyming magic. Can you figure out what she's been up to?

> ### Example:
> She turns a royal guy into a piece of jewelry.
> Answer: <u>king</u> is turned into <u>ring</u>

1. She turns an animal doctor into a plane.

   _____ is turned into _____

2. She turns a group of musicians into a group of fingers.

   _____ is turned into _____

3. She turns a child into a bottle top.

   _____ is turned into _____

4. She turns guys into a writing tool.

   _____ is turned into _____

5. She turns a silly person into something you dive into.

   _____ is turned into _____

6. She turns a sports lover into an aluminum container.

   _____ is turned into _____

7. She turns a horse racer into an ice sport.

_____ is turned into _____

8. She turns a man into a pesky insect
   (that quickly befriends the witch!).

_____ is turned into _____

9. She turns a financial advisor into an
   oil-carrying truck.

_____ is turned into _____

10. She turns a bride's favorite guy into her
    favorite flying tool.

_____ is turned into _____

Fractured Fairy Tales

Think of your favorite fairy tales to figure out the titles of these stories. All you have to do is fill in the parts of each letter that are missing.

Hint: Write the alphabet. Look for missing parts in the letters you've written.

THE LITTLE MERMAID

HANSEL AND GRETEL

SNOW WHITE AND THE SEVEN DWARFS

RUMPELSTILTSKIN

RED RIDING HOOD

A V E R Y
H A P P Y
B I R T H
D A Y T O
Y O O O O

List the words you find here:

dairy

What's in the Box?

**How many words can you find in the gift above?
Start with any letter. To form a word, switch directions
by moving left, right, up, down, or diagonally.**

Baker's Dozen

**Find 13 baked goods hidden in this tall tale.
Look in the middle of words or put the end of one
word with the beginning of the next.**

The cook I educated makes me dinner a lot. "Is the hot cobweb ready yet?" I ask when I walk into her restaurant. "Almost," she says, as she pours Tabasco neatly over my dish. Then she throws an earmuff in. She covers it with tapioca ketchup. She adds a tomato asteroid. Then she flattens the whole dish with a steamroller. Finally, she tops it with a piece of dragon tongue. Next thing I know, she covers the food in firecrackers, lights them, and I eat. She follows that with an amoeba gelatin dessert. To top it off, she offers me a delicious popcorn, breadfruit snack. Home I return, overjoyed. My favorite cook is dancing in the dough, nutty and very sweet.

CYFOTL?

(Can You Figure Out These Lists?)

No, it's not an eye chart.
Each letter stands for something in a list.

> Example:
> "MTWTFSS are week in, week out,"
> **means**
> Monday, Tuesday, Wednesday, Thursday,
> Friday, Saturday, Sunday!

RSSH can't keep the postman away!

WSSF are always in season.

ROYGBIV are somewhere over the rainbow.

JFMAMJJASOND come once a year.

MVEMJSUNP take up space.

DDPVCCDB offer Santa a ride.

BEAGLE	CORGI	POINTER	SETTER
BULLDOG	DEERHOUND	POMERANIAN	SPANIEL
CHIHUAHUA	FOXHOUND	POODLE	TERRIER
CHOW	MALTESE	PUG	WHIPPET
COLLIE	MASTIFF	SCHNAUZER	

```
E  P  Y  S  I  G  R  O  C  M  Z  P
I  F  R  E  Z  U  A  N  H  C  S  U
B  F  S  T  T  E  R  R  I  E  R  G
S  I  P  T  B  C  E  D  H  W  T  B
E  T  A  E  E  O  T  N  U  S  G  U
S  S  N  R  A  L  N  U  A  V  W  L
E  A  I  H  G  L  I  O  H  E  H  L
T  M  E  E  L  I  O  H  U  L  I  D
L  L  L  I  E  E  P  R  A  D  P  O
A  N  A  I  N  A  R  E  M  O  P  G
M  J  C  H  O  W  H  E  M  O  E  N
F  O  X  H  O  U  N  D  L  P  T  I
```

Doggie Bag

You should get a "ruff" idea of what this word search is about by the title. Listed words go up, down, backward, and forward.

Signs of Spring

**You have one minute to find ten squares
that look exactly like this:**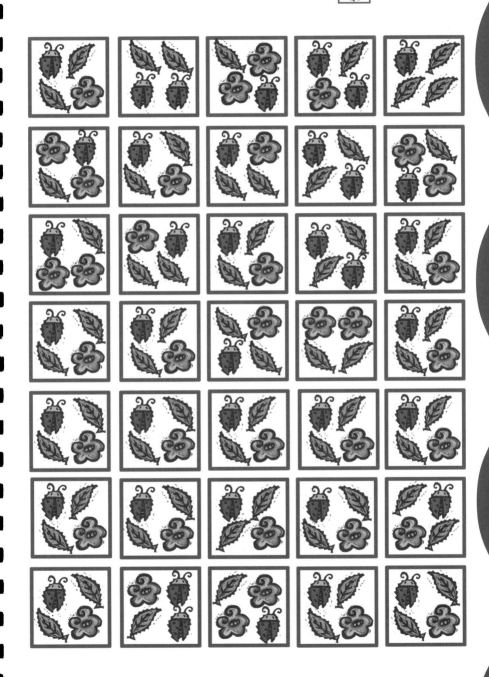

Repeat That

Each of the following words ends in the same word. Use the clues to fill in the blanks and complete the words.

NO! NO! NO!

An herb _ _ _ _ _ _ _ N O

It's a gamble to go here _ _ _ _ _ N O

A tile in a game _ _ _ _ N O

A horned animal _ _ _ N O

Japanese clothing _ _ _ _ N O

A tan horse _ _ _ _ _ _ _ N O

An exploding mountain _ _ _ _ _ _ N O

A large musical instrument _ _ _ N O

HA! HA! HA!

Hawaiian greeting _ _ _ H A

Washington's wife _ _ _ _ _ H A

Largest city in Nebraska _ _ _ H A

One + One = One

**Add together each of the defined words to get
a whole new word.**

Example:

a small insect *ant*

+ run away to get married *elope*

= a swift wild animal *antelope*

---

a healed wound _____

+ allow _____

= a bright red color _____

---

to pull something along
the ground _____

+ the opposite of off _____

= a mythical creature _____

---

a tool for filling up a
bike tire _____

+ relatives _____

= a gourd _____

Animal Magic

Work your magic and you can turn ordinary things into animals. Change the first letter of the word and presto!

> ## Example:
> Change a container into a sly, bushy-tailed animal.
> Answer: _Box_ becomes _fox_

1. Change a water vehicle into a farm animal.

   _____ becomes _____

2. Change something you wear on your head into a rodent.

   _____ becomes _____

3. Change a dead tree trunk into a canine.

   _____ becomes _____

4. Change a place you live into a small, gnawing mammal.

_____ becomes _____

5. Change a sports stick into a furry pet.

_____ becomes _____

6. Change a plate into a swimmer.

_____ becomes _____

7. Change your front yard into a small deer.

_____ becomes _____

8. Change a magician into a reptile.

_____ becomes _____

Chew on This!

Bounce Back!

You drop a perfectly inflated kickball off a ten-story building onto a cement sidewalk. But it only bounces back up a few inches. Why?

Just Do It!

Some people like word searches, and some have other hobbies! See if you can find something you like to do. Listed words go up, down, backward, forward, and diagonally.

```
A O J L S P O T T E R Y
A R C H E R Y T F L O G
B I T C O O K I N G G X
V G I N V E S T I N G T
C A T G N I D D E L S D
R M A O G N I D I R A S
A I T G N I X O B N H I
F P T C I S U M C S I N
T E I A T O S I C D K G
S T N F C K N E R R I I
F S G R A G R P H A N N
S Y R T N E P R A C G G
```

ACTING	HIKING
ARCHERY	INVESTING
ART	MUSIC
BOXING	ORIGAMI
CARDS	PETS
CARPENTRY	POTTERY
CHESS	RIDING
COOKING	SINGING
CRAFTS	SLEDDING
DANCING	TATTING
GOLF	

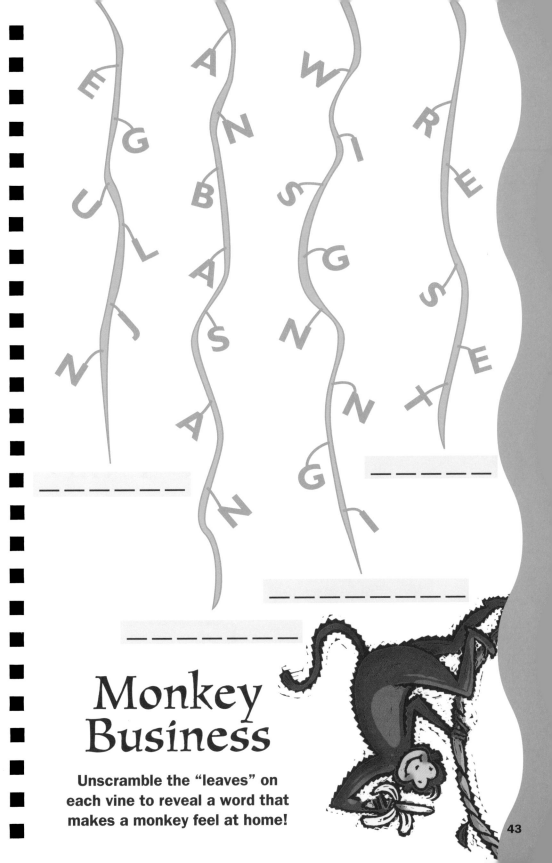

Monkey Business

Unscramble the "leaves" on each vine to reveal a word that makes a monkey feel at home!

What's found on a farm,
has funny-looking ears,
and crows in the morning?

A young cornfield

What's small,
gold colored, and
swims in fish ponds?

A frog wearing lots
of jewelry!

Riddle
Me This

What are warm and soft
and found on beds?

Cats!

What's brown,
grows underground,
and has many eyes?

A colony of gophers

Botched-Up Books

The Botched-Up Books publisher hoped to create bestsellers by changing the titles of award-winning children's books. Draw a line from the made-up book title to its real title. The first one has been done for you.

1. Simple Girl Reaches Top Shelf

2. A Month Gone

3. Pal, Not Friend

4. Directional Tag

5. Confused Woman with Paperwork

6. Dirty (Cough!) Place (Cough!)

Missing May

Out of the Dust

From the Mixed-Up Files of Mrs. Basil E. Frankweiler

The Westing Game

Sarah, Plain and Tall

Bud, Not Buddy

Mixed Messages

Using the definitions shown, figure out the first two words. Then put their letters in the right spaces to spell a third word.

Hint: Start with the easiest word, even if it's the third word.

Example:
A thinker

$$\underset{5}{B}\ \underset{1}{R}\ \underset{2}{A}\ \underset{3}{I}\ \underset{4}{N}$$

Expression of pain

$$\underset{6}{O}\ \underset{7}{W}$$

Many colors in the sky

$$\underset{1}{R}\ \underset{2}{A}\ \underset{3}{I}\ \underset{4}{N}\ \underset{5}{B}\ \underset{6}{O}\ \underset{7}{W}$$

A grain often baked into flakes

$$\overline{\ \ }_{1}\ \overline{\ \ }_{5}\ \overline{\ \ }_{3}\ \overline{\ \ }_{7}$$

A grain cooked for breakfast

$$\overline{\ \ }_{6}\ \overline{\ \ }_{2}\ \overline{\ \ }_{4}\ \overline{\ \ }_{8}$$

Animated TV shows

$$\overline{\ \ }_{1}\ \overline{\ \ }_{2}\ \overline{\ \ }_{3}\ \overline{\ \ }_{4}\ \overline{\ \ }_{5}\ \overline{\ \ }_{6}\ \overline{\ \ }_{7}\ \overline{\ \ }_{8}$$

What you are when no one else is there

$$\overline{\ \ }_{1}\ \overline{\ \ }_{2}\ \overline{\ \ }_{4}\ \overline{\ \ }_{7}\ \overline{\ \ }_{9}$$

A cat's weapon

$$\overline{\ \ }_{8}\ \overline{\ \ }_{3}\ \overline{\ \ }_{6}\ \overline{\ \ }_{5}$$

Once-a-week money for helping out

$$\overline{\ \ }_{1}\ \overline{\ \ }_{2}\ \overline{\ \ }_{3}\ \overline{\ \ }_{4}\ \overline{\ \ }_{5}\ \overline{\ \ }_{6}\ \overline{\ \ }_{7}\ \overline{\ \ }_{8}\ \overline{\ \ }_{9}$$

What you are when you're finished

$$\overline{}_{7} \quad \overline{}_{4} \quad \overline{}_{5} \quad \overline{}_{2}$$

Something you eat three times a day

$$\overline{}_{3} \quad \overline{}_{8} \quad \overline{}_{6} \quad \overline{}_{1}$$

A summertime drink

$$\overline{}_{1} \quad \overline{}_{2} \quad \overline{}_{3} \quad \overline{}_{4} \quad \overline{}_{5} \quad \overline{}_{6} \quad \overline{}_{7} \quad \overline{}_{8}$$

Gretel's companion

$$\overline{}_{5} \quad \overline{}_{6} \quad \overline{}_{7} \quad \overline{}_{9} \quad \overline{}_{1} \quad \overline{}_{2}$$

An animal companion in your house

$$\overline{}_{4} \quad \overline{}_{3} \quad \overline{}_{8}$$

Big-eared, giant animals

$$\overline{}_{1} \quad \overline{}_{2} \quad \overline{}_{3} \quad \overline{}_{4} \quad \overline{}_{5} \quad \overline{}_{6} \quad \overline{}_{7} \quad \overline{}_{8} \quad \overline{}_{9}$$

start

finish

Go for the Gold!

Race through this maze to win the gold at the end.

48

Castle Crisis

Six dragons kidnapped six princesses and kept them each in a separate castle.
Luckily, the princesses escaped. Not one princess crossed the escape path of another princess!
Can you figure out each path?

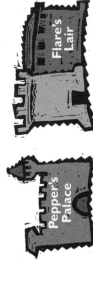

Pepper's Palace

Flare's Lair

Hotbreath's Hangout

Kindle's Kingdom

Blaze's Berth

Fume's Flat

Fume's Exit

Pepper's Exit

Blaze's Exit

Flare's Exit

Kindle's Exit

Hotbreath's Exit

Just Passing Through

Without lifting your pencil from the page, draw only four straight lines with at least one of them passing through each of these nine dots.

● ● ●

● ● ●

● ● ●

Chew on This!

Trouble

Someone's in trouble, and she's left you a message. Read the message to find out what's wrong— before it's too late!

HELPIMTRAPPEDINSIDE
THISMIRROR

What has 22 legs
and goes crunch,
crunch, crunch?

A soccer team eating
potato chips

What has a back
and four legs, and
people sit on it?

A horse

What's made of
sticks and mud and
found high in a tree?

A beaver dam after a
flood

What has eight legs
and eats flies?

Two frogs

Riddle Me This

Stormy Subject

Fit the weather words into the grid below. It's a breeze!

Blizzard	Drizzle	Hurricane
Breeze	Frost	Monsoon
Cloudburst	Gale	Rain
Cyclone	Hail	Thunder

Brain Benders

Don't lose your sense of direction! These teasers might be tricky.

On the Right Hand
What can you hold in
your right hand that your friend
can't hold in her right hand?

_____

SOOZ OIHO
Can you read this sentence?

SOOZ OIHO NI WIMS MON SMONNIW XIS

_____

Animal Farm

Try this a-moo-sing word search! Listed words go up,
down, backward, forward, and diagonally.

```
C H B W P I L E M A C N
H H E Z U L E R R I U Q
S A A B M P I G H H I O
R J V M A K Y L L A M A
E I E R E B N N Z R K E
I G R R A L O U N E P K
N M A R E U E O M U I A
D C O L T G G O N P B N
E X L I O N D A N M I S
E N E T T I K A J A W H
R Y O F A W N T B R Q F
C L L A E S K K R C A T
```

BABOON	KITTEN
BADGER	LION
BEAVER	LLAMA
BUNNY	LYNX
CAMEL	MARE
CAT	PIG
CHAMELEON	PUMA
COLT	RAM
FAWN	REINDEER
HARE	SEAL
JAGUAR	SNAKE

Patriotic Pyramid

**Wave your pencil and change "A" to "American!"
Just add one letter in each step, then follow the clues
to rearrange the letters into a new word.**

A

__ __ Old-fashioned term for "mother"

__ __ __ A body part

__ __ __ __ Mama horse

__ __ __ __ __ After raw milk sets, this comes to the top

__ __ __ __ __ __ A photographer's tool

__ __ __ __ __ __ __ The United States of . . .

A M E R I C A N

What's in the Box?

How many words can you find in the gift below?
Start with any letter. To form a word, switch directions
by moving left, right, up, down, or diagonally.

Bzzz

Springtime
Buzzzz

B	U	T	T	E
R	F	L	I	E
S	A	N	D	B
U	M	B	L	E
B	E	E	Z	Z

List the words you find here:

Clover to You!

Follow the lines to find the meaning of each flower.

Clover	Faithful
Daisy	Friendship
Dandelion	Good luck
Forget-Me-Not	Innocent
Iris	Love
Pansy	Modest
Red Rose	Proud
Sunflower	Thoughtful
Violet	True love

Hold the Line

**Draw these tough shapes without
lifting your pencil from the paper or retracing lines.**

Hint: Start and end where three lines connect.

I Have a Code!

Sage and Hope like writing messages to each other— in code. Can you figure out what they're saying?

PIG LATIN

Sage: atwhay ouldway ouyay oday fiay ouyay awsay ay luebay lephanteay?

Hope: iay ouldway eerchay tiay puay!

ONG

Hope: Whongy dongo yongou thongink dong-yongins longove tongo plongay ongin songalt wongatonger?

Sage: Bongecongause pongepponger wonga-tonger mongakes thongem snongeeze!

Fun Money

1. Arrange four nickels like this:

Touching just two of the nickels, change them to look like this:

2. Arrange four nickels on a sheet of paper like this:

Touching none of the coins, change all the heads to tails and all the tails to heads.

Cross Country

**Can you travel from New Jersey to Arizona
without crossing any lines?**

start

finish

Riddle Me This

What travels long
distances over mountains
and through valleys,
is made mostly of water,
and has fish in it?

A bear!

So, how many mistakes
are there in this sentence?
She sells seeshells buy
the see sure.

None. Not in "this
sentence." In the next
sentence, though, there
are four misspelled words.

If 18 kids get on a bus,
and at the next stop,
eight get off, how many
kids are left on the bus?

It depends on
how many kids were
already on the bus when
the 18 kids got on.

What has eight legs and
walks on webs?

Four ducks!

Body Language

Find all the body-related terms in this word search,
and you'll feel good from head to toe. Listed words go
up, down, backward, and forward.

```
Q  O  U  V  L  E  E  H  W  O  R  B
S  X  W  O  B  L  E  H  U  T  Y  T
G  L  M  V  I  I  X  D  Y  O  M  A
N  B  M  H  R  G  H  O  J  O  M  O
U  B  R  L  I  A  N  E  O  T  U  R
L  E  A  F  T  M  S  T  W  H  T  H
F  L  E  L  E  E  P  D  A  L  M  T
E  L  R  A  E  N  E  R  V  E  S  K
Y  Y  O  C  F  T  C  H  E  S  T  E
E  P  F  M  M  S  P  I  L  J  E
D  K  C  A  B  S  T  O  M  A  C  H
I  E  P  I  P  D  N  I  W  T  C  C
```

BACK	LIGAMENTS
BELLY	LIPS
BROW	LUNGS
CALF	NERVES
CHEEK	RIB
CHEST	STOMACH
ELBOW	THROAT
EYE	TOENAIL
FEET	TOOTH
FOREARM	TUMMY
HEEL	WINDPIPE

"C" You This Weekend!

Across

1. Sunday morning funnies
4. Preparing food to eat
5. Rolling hair makes it _____.
6. What you do at a birthday party
7. Traveling amusement park
8. A music show in a stadium
9. You do this to others when you play tag.
10. Make looped stitches with a hooked needle.
14. Another name for movie theater
15. Game with red and black disks
17. Game with king and queen
18. Fancy pen-and-ink writing
19. Go here to see the ocean.
22. CD stands for _____ disk.
23. 52 of these = 100s of games
24. Join a _____ or create one.
26. Party where shell food is cooked on the beach

27. If your room's a mess, you might be asked to do this.
28. Talks with pals
29. A bike

Down

1. This boat is easy to tip!
2. To gather similar objects
3. Saturday morning TV
4. Boat trip
6. Traveling animal acts with clowns
8. Some religions are practiced here.
9. Small diner
11. Chocolate drink that's great on cold days
12. Tool to take pictures
13. Sometimes you need to organize this.
14. To "surf," you need this.
15. A _____ often depends on help from volunteers.
16. Arts and _____
19. Bake these a dozen at a time.
20. Words and pictures glued randomly on a surface
21. A favorite kind of pet
25. To play _____, you toss a ball back and forth.
26. Deadline for being inside

You'll "C" there's one weekend activity missing from this puzzle—crosswords!

Traveling Letters

Move the letters in each word down the alphabet the same number of letters to find another word. If you move all the letters in COLD down the alphabet three spaces— C (DEF), O (PQR), L (MNO), D (EFG)—you'd get FROG! From the blue word, can you figure out the new word?

1. How you feel when you're unhappy

AIL  _s_ _a_ ___

2. Relatives are also called kin_____.

IRON ___ ___ ___ ___

3. A little, annoying flying bug

TANG ___ ___ ___ ___

4. What you do at night

BUNNY ___ ___ ___ ___ ___

5. This animal looks a little like a person.

PET ___ ___ ___

6. How Santa feels when he's full of cheer

CHEER ___ ___ ___ ___ ___

Here's a little help!

A B C D E F G H I

J K L M N O P Q R

S T U V W X Y Z

Four Minus Four Equals . . . Eight?

STOP! Can you take four of something away from this square and leave eight?

Brain Benders

See if you can figure out how these teasers shape up.

Square It Away

There are a lot of squares in this grid. Can you figure out how many?

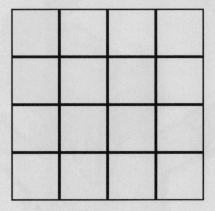

Twist and Shout

Each word below has a partner in a circle other than the one it's in. For instance, one answer is "twist and shout."
Find the other 11.

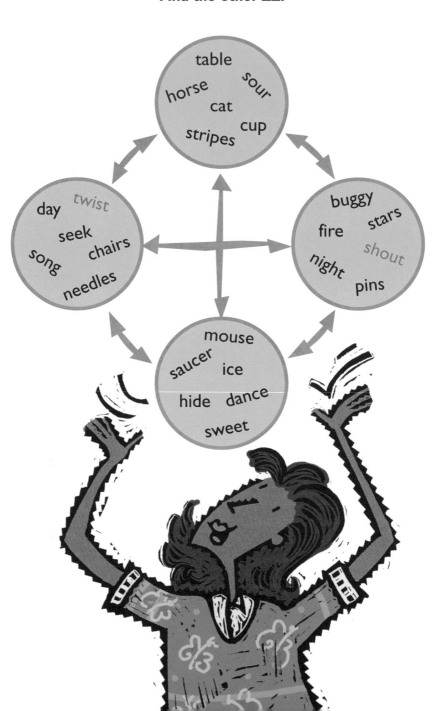

table
horse
sour
cat
cup
stripes

day
twist
seek
chairs
song
needles

buggy
fire
stars
shout
night
pins

mouse
saucer
ice
hide
dance
sweet

twist and *shout*

.... and ....

.... and ....

.... and ....

.... and ....

.... and ....

.... and ....

.... and ....

.... and ....

.... and ....

.... and ....

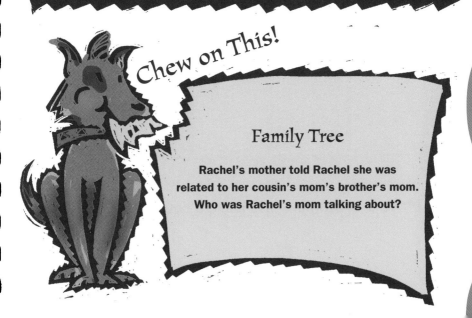

Chew on This!

Family Tree

Rachel's mother told Rachel she was related to her cousin's mom's brother's mom. Who was Rachel's mom talking about?

Tricky Toothpicks!

Pull out your toothpicks to try these puzzling plays.

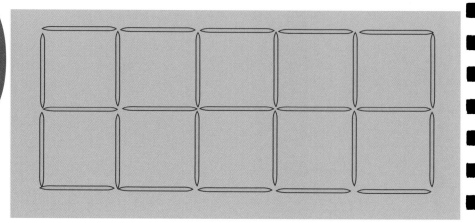

1. Remove 3 toothpicks from these squares and leave 10 squares.

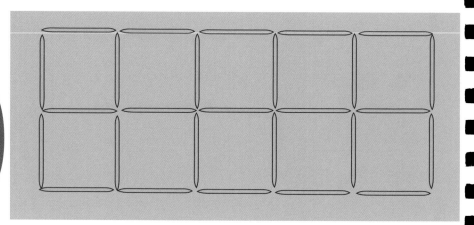

2. Move 3 toothpicks and leave 8 squares.

3. Move 3 toothpicks to create 4 squares.

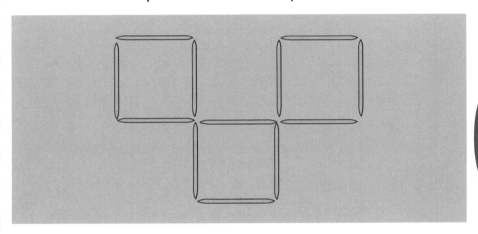

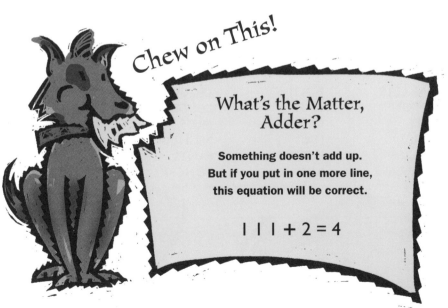

Chew on This!

What's the Matter, Adder?

**Something doesn't add up.
But if you put in one more line,
this equation will be correct.**

1 1 1 + 2 = 4

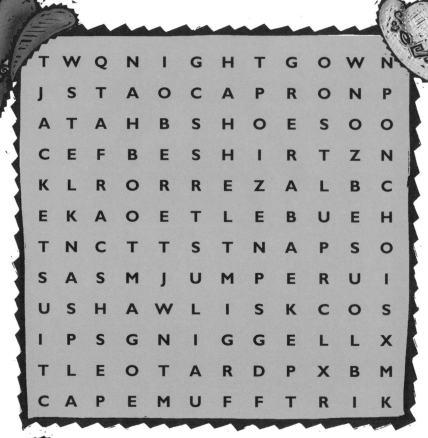

```
T W Q N I G H T G O W N
J S T A O C A P R O N P
A T A H B S H O E S O O
C E F B E S H I R T Z N
K L R O R R E Z A L B C
E K A O E T L E B U E H
T N C T T S T N A P S O
S A S M J U M P E R U I
U S H A W L I S K C O S
I P S G N I G G E L L X
T L E O T A R D P X B M
C A P E M U F F T R I K
```

Clothes Call

**Try this stylish word search. Listed words
go up, down, backward, and forward.**

ANKLETS	BOOT	LEGGINGS	SCARF
APRON	CAPE	LEOTARD	SHAWL
BELT	COAT	MUFF	SHIRT
BERET	HAT	NIGHTGOWN	SHOES
BLAZER	JACKET	PANTS	SOCKS
BLOUSE	JUMPER	PONCHO	SUIT

Repeat That

Each of the following words ends in the same word. Use the clues to fill in the blanks and complete the words.

DING DING DING

When two people unite __ __ __ __ D I N G

Four walls and a roof __ __ __ __ __ D I N G

A dessert __ __ __ D I N G

A book activity __ __ __ __ D I N G

Joking and teasing __ __ __ __ D I N G

Slow down, you're … __ __ __ __ D I N G

SO SO SO

Mexican money __ __ S O

Caribbean music __ __ __ __ __ __ S O

Spanish artist __ __ __ __ __ S O

Too __ __ S O

Grover's Garden

To live in Grover's Garden, groundhogs agree not to enter, exit, or cross another's tunnel.
It took a bit of maneuvering, but eight groundhogs have made it work.
Can you draw a tunnel to each groundhog's exit?

Of "elephant,"
"rhinoceros," and
"hippopotamus,"
which has three syllables?

All of them have three syllables. Some have even more.

Where do knights, kings, and queens live?

In chess sets

Riddle Me This

What has four legs, a tail, and black-and-white stripes?

A horse in jail

Why won't zookeepers play games at the zoos?

Because there are too many cheetahs!

Face the Music

Fit these noteworthy types of music into the cross grid.

Ballad	Disco	Lullaby	Rock
Bluegrass	Fusion	Polka	Soul
Blues	Gospel	Pop	Swing
Country	Jazz	Rap	

Stop, Look, and Be A-mazed!

See if you can find your way through this maze.

start ↘

finish ↓

One, Two, Three!

**Each of these sayings needs a number or two to complete it.
(You'll find 5 ones, 6 twos, and 3 threes.)**

1. It takes _____ to start an argument.

2. _____ wrongs don't make a right.

3. All for _____ and _____ for all.

4. _____ is company, _____ is a crowd.

5. A bird in the hand is worth _____ in the bush.

6. There are _____ sides to every story.

7. _____ heads are better than _____.

8. And baby makes _____.

9. It takes _____ to know _____.

10. Fish and visitors begin to smell after _____ days.

MCYFOTL?

(More Can You
Figure Out These Lists?)

**Each capital letter stands
for something in a list.
See page 35 for an example.**

OTTFFSSENTET work around the clock.

DRMFSLTD strike the right chord.

RGYBO keep Crayola in business.

CVS make a great triple dip.

PNDQ put a jingle in your pocket.

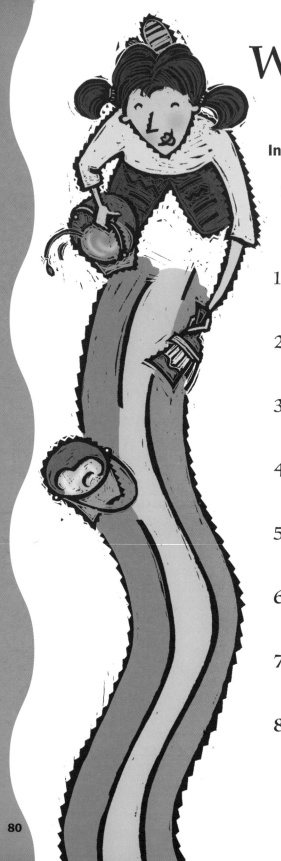

What's the Color?

In each of the lists below, all of the words come from the letters in the name of a color.

1. ape, heap, cap

2. are, mare, care

3. tan, manage, tea

4. live, rise, vise

5. ail, call, ill

6. big, gee, beg

7. ant, great, tire

8. tour, quiet, sour

What's in the Box?

**How many words can you find in the boxes below?
Start with any letter. To make a word, switch directions
by moving left, right, up, down, or diagonally.**

Summer
Fun

```
S C H O O
      S O U
L I
T A N D S   U
U M M E R   S
S H E R E   R
```

List the words you find here:

Count Your Q's . . .

See if you can count all the Q's on this page.

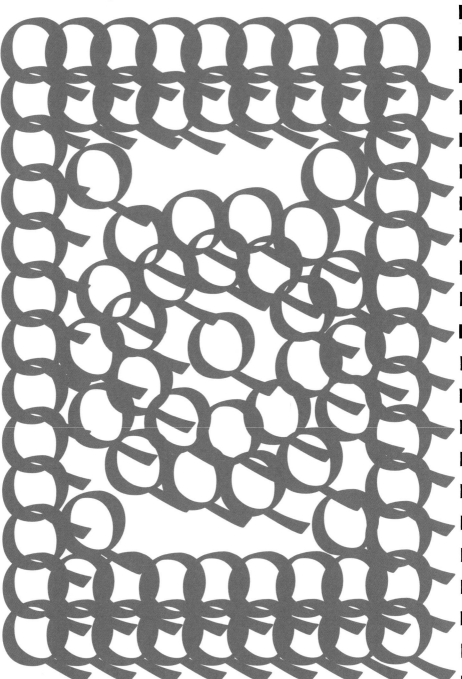

Hint: Place a pencil dot inside each Q or cone as you count it.

. . . and Cones!

Now cool down by counting all the ice cream cones.

ABC, 123

Fill in the blanks with three consecutive letters to find words that are school related.

School Stuff

E _ _ E _ E _ T A R Y

_ _ L A _ K B O A R _

Q U _ R T E R _ _ A _ K

_ L P H A _ E T I _ A L

Puppy Puzzler

The judges chose four finalists at the Barksville Dog Show. Unfortunately, they have confused which name goes with which breed. Using the clues, fill in the chart to help solve the problem. Finally, guess the name of the dog who won the show. We've given the first clue to you.

	Pepper	Prince	Prancer	Pearl
Great Dane				no
Collie				no
Chihuahua				no
Siberian Husky	no	no	no	yes

1. Pearl sometimes pulls a sled.
2. Prince is the smallest dog.
3. Prancer's breed starts with a C.
4. The collie won the blue ribbon.

Silly Sentences

These sentences will actually make sense if you put the same letter in each blank. See page 8 for an example.

____ive-____oot ____annie ____ights ____irey ____lames ____rom ____loating ____erries.

____eddy ____eased ____he ____wins ____ill ____hey ____ired. ____hanks, ____eddy!

____rim, ____rave ____hosts ____rasp ____race's ____littering, ____listening ____own. ____ail ____asps, "____ross!"

____owena ____arely ____ecords ____ap.
____oxie ____egularly ____eplays ____ock.

____lena ____ats ____ggplant ____very ____vening.

____ad ____abel ____ade ____eek ____andy
____arch ____any ____iles. "____arch, ____andy,
____arch!" ____uttered ____abel. ____andy
____erely ____oaned.

Ballet Play

If you love puzzles or like to dance,
solve this rhyming crossword when you have the chance.

ACROSS

1. These shoes of satin or leather make you feel light as a feather.

3. To warm your muscles, go to a barre. Just don't _____ too far.

7. Wear makeup for the _____ to see—especially from the balcony!

8. A dancer's body and face show a lot of style and _____.

10. A _____ will hold hair in place and keep it off shoulders and face.

11. To help your arm stay supple and flow, support your wrist and _____.

13. This isn't surprising news: ballet dancers wear_____.

14. By using body and face to react, dancers don't need to speak to _____.

16. A classic ballerina has a long _____, so find a mirror to give yours a check.

18. You need strong _____ to go up on toe. Until you build strength, you'd better stay low!

20. If you're ready for _____ shoes, your teacher will give you the news.

21. Nothing is better, nothing sweeter, than to dance in a crowded _____.

22. It may seem like a curse, but before a show, you must _____.

23. It's a popular color, many think. When choosing a tutu, many like _____.

24. To prevent the slipping of their shoes, dancers rub them with this goo.

25. You look like a ballet star when you're stretching at the _____.

26. Slippers do not come with these, so ask someone to add them, please.

DOWN

1. It may sound silly or simply absurd, but in this ballet, the princess is a bird!

2. Ballerinas show grace and _____. When they dance, they don't make noise.

4. This ballet has an army of mice and sugar-plum fairies who are really nice.

5. When you need to reach those heights, you'll feel more comfy wearing _____.

6. Most ballets have simple _____, so dancers have room for pirouettes.

9. You don't have to be the prettiest or smartest to be a dancer who's a great _____.

12. To be a prima _____ is a dream come true. Someday it may happen to you!

15. When you aren't sure what to do, this person will give you a clue.

17. If you need to do this, say it the French way: grand plié or demi-plié.

19. Go _____ by _____ to learn each position, and soon you'll be ready to audition!

22. If *The Nutcracker* is your goal, then Clara is a wonderful _____.

24. Be sure your ribbons are tied right. They might _____ if they're too tight.

Animal Magic

**Change the first letter of a word and presto!
You've created an animal.**

1. Change a dinner into a fat sea animal.

   _____ becomes _____

2. Change fabric into a very slow animal.

   _____ becomes _____

3. Change a fruit into a wild animal.

   _____ becomes _____

4. Change a street into an amphibian.

   _____ becomes _____

5. Change misty weather into a fat farm animal.

   _____ becomes _____

6. Change a glove into a soft, furry animal.

   _____ becomes _____

7. Change a fake hair piece into something that squeals.

_____ becomes _____

8. Change a fruit spread into a sheepish guy.

_____ becomes _____

Chew on This!

Spooky Stuff?

Seven cattle ranchers rode into
a ghost town one day. But while they
were there, the town had no men
or horses. How can this be?

Just One Word

Can you use all of these letters to spell just one word?

d e j n o o r s t u w

_____

Wrong, Wrong, Wrong!

There are three mistakes in this pearagraph. Can you fined them all?

_____

A Longer Word

You can write the longest word you know, and when you turn to the answer page, you'll find a longer word than you wrote. What do you think you'll read there?

_____

Brain Benders

Twist your brain around this word play.

Compound Fractures

Find the one word that turns each of these sets into compound words.

day_____

flash_____

flood_____

head_____

moon_____

search_____

sky_____

spot_____

sun_____

hand_____

match_____

text_____

work_____

year_____

eye_____

foot_____

snow_____

soft_____

Beach Diary

Dig around for the answers to these clues. The last letter of each answer is the first letter of the next one.

Dear Diary,

This vacation, I went to the beach with my family.

We tossed beach 1. _ _ _ _ _ S at each other,

made 2. S _ _ _ _ _ _ _ _ _ _ _ _ using my little

sister's pail, and searched along the water's edge for

3. _ _ _ _ _ _ _ _ _ _. After a few hours, everyone

climbed under the umbrella for a break from the sun. I

just slathered on more 4. _ _ _ _ _ _ _ _ _ _, then

walked over to help kids put up a 5. _ _ _ _ for beach

volleyball. I played for a while, then wanted to be alone

to daydream. I hunted for sea stars and sea urchins in a

6. _ _ _ _ _ _ _ _ _ _, and I walked around two

blue 7. _ _ _ _ _ _ _ _ _ _, where I found a round,

white 8. _ _ _ _ _ _ _ _ _ _ _ _ bleached

from the sun. At the end of the day, I joined my

family and we all laid on towels, listening to

music on my 9. _ _ _ _ _ _ _. It felt so great to

be 10. _ _ _ _ _ _ _ _ after a long winter.

Winding Words

One word from the list below will fit best between the two words on the line. The first one has been done for you.

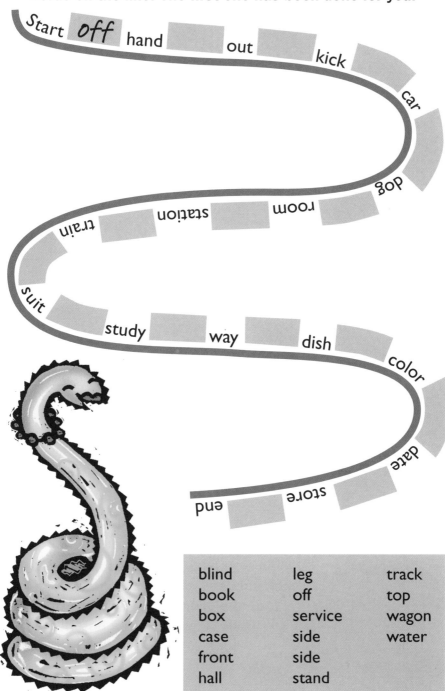

Start **off** hand ⬜ out ⬜ kick ⬜ car ⬜ dog ⬜ room ⬜ station ⬜ train ⬜ suit ⬜ study ⬜ way ⬜ dish ⬜ color ⬜ date ⬜ store ⬜ end

Hint: Fill in the words you know, then place the extra words to see where they fit best.

blind	leg	track
book	off	top
box	service	wagon
case	side	water
front	side	
hall	stand	

1. I Can See the Weekend!

2. Lady Werewolf

3. Space Exercises

4. Sewing Kit Needed

5. 158 Trillion ... 159 Trillion ...

6. Take This, Please!

7. Cluckman Is Kind

Dear Mr. Henshaw

The Giver

Holes

Number the Stars

Walk Two Moons

The View from Saturday

Julie of the Wolves

Botched-Up Books

The Botched-Up Books publisher had such success with her previous book line that she changed a few more titles. Draw a line from the botched book to the correct title.

Star Power

**Follow the lines to find the name that
each of these famous people was given at birth.**

Elton John	Kenneth Brian Edmonds
Cher	Reginald Kenneth Dwight
Tom Cruise	Margaret Hyra
Meg Ryan	Thomas C. Mapother
Whoopi Goldberg	Caryn Johnson
Enya	David Adkins
Babyface	Cherilyn Sarkesían
Sting	Gordon Sumner
Sinbad	Eithne Ni Bhraonain

One + One = ^Another One

**Add together each of the defined words
to get a whole new word.**

to shout _____

+ what you say when you
feel pain _____
_____

= a color _____

a light brown color _____

+ to leave _____
_____

= a dance _____

an announcement of
something for sale _____

+ a type of woman's clothing _____
_____

= a building's location _____

a vehicle _____

+ an animal pal _____
_____
= a floor covering _____

the opposite of "him" _____

+ a piece of jewelry _____
_____
= a small fish _____

a young dog _____

+ a household animal _____
_____
= a type of doll _____

the ocean _____

+ a father's boy _____
_____
= part of the year _____

another name for dad _____

+ a yellow veggie _____
_____
= a white fluffy snack _____

Mixed Messages

Using the definitions, figure out the first two words. Next, put their letters in the right spaces to spell a third word. See page 46 for an example.

When you're not wet, you are

$$\overline{}\ \overline{}\ \overline{}$$
6   3   8

Repeating a behavior is called a

$$\overline{}\ \overline{}\ \overline{}\ \overline{}\ \overline{}$$
5   7   1   2   4

A once-a-year special day for you

$$\overline{}\ \overline{}\ \overline{}\ \overline{}\ \overline{}\ \overline{}\ \overline{}\ \overline{}$$
1   2   3   4   5   6   7   8

She marks your paper to find your score

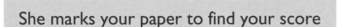
1   2   3   5   10   11

One-twelfth of a year

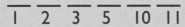
6   7   4   8   9

An older relative

1   2   3   4   5   6   7   8   9   10   11

If you get sunburned, your skin could

$$\overline{}\ \overline{}\ \overline{}\ \overline{}$$
$$5\quad 8\quad 4\quad 2$$

A person who figures out puzzles

$$\overline{}\ \overline{}\ \overline{}\ \overline{}\ \overline{}\ \overline{}$$
$$1\quad 6\quad 2\quad 7\quad 3\quad 9$$

A fun all-nighter with your pals

$$\overline{}\ \overline{}\ \overline{}\ \overline{}\ \overline{}\ \overline{}\ \overline{}\ \overline{}\ \overline{}$$
$$1\quad 2\quad 3\quad 4\quad 5\quad 6\quad 7\quad 8\quad 9$$

Chew on This!

Leg Work

You crawl under a table
and see ten legs, not counting yours.
How many people are sitting
at the table?

Music Box

Play around with this musical word search. Listed words go up, down, backward, forward, and diagonally.

```
Y S P F T E P M U R T K
E A I E H S B B O N G O
N X C L A T A O J N A B
O H C E R E L W M U R D
H O O L P N A F E R Y L
P R L U C A L L I O P E
O N O K T T A U O E P G
L O B U E S I T O I F U
Y N T L N A K E P J V I
X A U U R C A G G Q N T
F I B T O M A R A C A A
D P A E C B S I T A R R
```

BAGPIPE	CORNET	LYRE	TRUMPET
BALALAIKA	DRUM	MARACA	TUBA
BANJO	FLUTE	PIANO	UKULELE
BONGO	GUITAR	PICCOLO	VIOLA
CALLIOPE	HARP	SAXHORN	XYLOPHONE
CASTANETS	LUTE	SITAR	

Who Likes Who?

Friends Jasmine, Karina, Lindsey, and Morgan each have a boy they like but can't exactly remember who likes who. Can you help? Here's what they do remember:

	Lancaster	James	Logan	Jason
Jasmine				
Karina				
Lindsey				
Morgan				

1. Morgan likes a boy who is called by his nickname, Jim.

2. Jasmine likes a boy with a name that starts with the same letter as hers.

3. You can divide Karina's friend's name into two syllables.

103

Safari Search

Fill in the blanks with the name of an animal to
make a word. Add that animal to your list on page 105.
You should discover five different animals.

1. R E _ _ _ _ E

2. D E _ _ _ _ E

3. D E D I _ _ _ _ E

4. _ _ _ _ _ D

5. _ _ _ M E N T

6. W O M _ _ _ _

7. G _ _ _ _ E

8. L O _ _ _ E

9. _ _ _ E O N

10. S _ _ _ _ OT

11. NAR _ _ _ _ E

12. DELI _ _ _ _ E

13. MA _ _ _ _ HON

14. UN _ _ _ _ _ ABLE

Your list of animals

_____

_____

_____

_____

_____

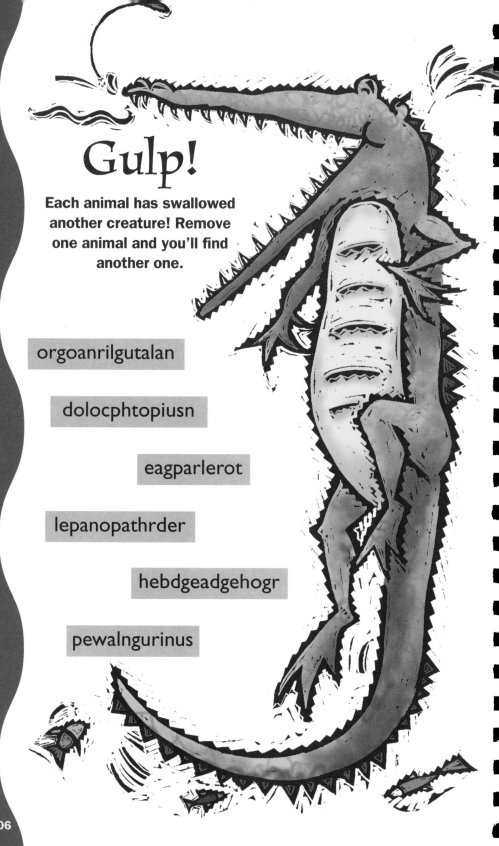

Gulp!

Each animal has swallowed another creature! Remove one animal and you'll find another one.

orgoanrilgutalan

dolocphtopiusn

eagparlerot

lepanopathrder

hebdgeadgehogr

pewalngurinus

very Tricky Toothpicks!

You need toothpicks and your thinking cap for these teasers.

1. Remove 5 toothpicks from these 12 and leave 8.

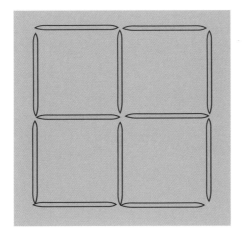

2. Remove 3 toothpicks and leave 6.

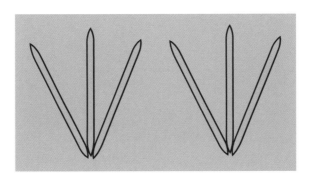

Sarah's Wacky Words

Sarah and her teacher enjoy joking around with each other. So when Ms. Witt passed out a questionnaire to the class, Sarah answered it in wacky words. Ms. Witt was able to figure it out. Can you?

Class Questionnaire

1. What reward do you get for all your studying?

AAAAAAAAAA

2. What do you want to do for a living?

the moo–I want BB–V V V V

3. What did you have for breakfast today?

bake N X

4. What should you try to eat for dinner?

$$\frac{Meal}{\triangle}$$

5. What are you looking forward to?

$$\frac{a \ sleep}{this \ weekend}$$

BEAUTY AND THE BEAST

THE UGLY DUCKLING

THE PRINCESS AND THE PEA

JACK AND THE BEANSTALK

Fractured Fairy Tales

Think of your favorite fairy tales to figure out the titles of these stories. All you have to do is fill in the parts of each letter that are missing.

ARTICHOKE	LEEKS
BEET	LENTIL
BROCCOLI	OKRA
CORN	OLIVE
DANDELION	PEA
EGGPLANT	PEPPER
FENNEL	POTATO
GARLIC	PUMPKIN
GHERKIN	RADISH
HOMINY	SHALLOT
KALE	TOMATO
KOHLRABI	YAM

```
D  P  E  R  O  H  O  M  I  N  Y  L
Y  A  U  K  O  H  L  R  A  B  I  K
Y  A  N  M  W  L  E  E  K  S  O  E
R  C  M  D  P  P  O  T  A  T  O  K
B  A  I  O  E  K  T  O  M  A  T  O
R  L  D  L  A  L  I  E  C  O  O  H
O  I  P  I  R  K  I  N  O  K  L  C
C  T  E  V  S  A  A  O  R  R  L  I
C  N  P  E  B  H  G  L  N  A  A  T
O  E  P  E  L  E  N  N  E  F  H  R
L  L  E  G  G  P  L  A  N  T  S  A
I  T  R  G  H  E  R  K  I  N  C  M
```

Veg Out

This word search is really good for you. Listed words go up, down, backward, forward, and diagonally.

Switch Witch Returns

The switch witch is back and she's made more changes.
Turn to page 30 to see an example of her handiwork.

1. She turns a parent's girl child into H_2O.

   _____ is turned into _____

2. She turns a husband's spouse into a tool that cuts.

   _____ is turned into _____

3. She turns a mini magical girl into a milking farm.

   _____ is turned into _____

4. She turns the actors in a play into the pole on a ship.

   _____ is turned into _____

5. She turns a robber into a small stream.

   _____ is turned into _____

6. Until finally, she turns herself (oops!) into a hole along a road. (Yea!)

   _____ is turned into _____

Extra Serving!

Each word below has a food-related partner in a circle other than the one it's in. Can you find all 12?

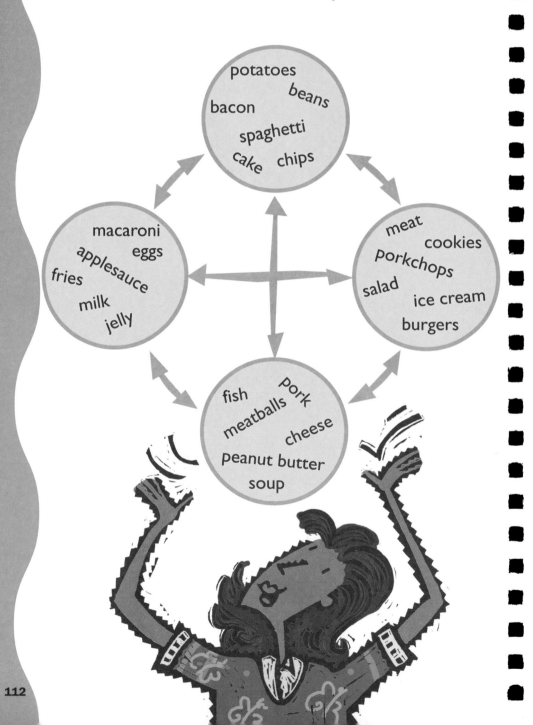

potatoes
beans
bacon
spaghetti
cake   chips

macaroni
eggs
applesauce
fries
milk
jelly

meat
cookies
porkchops
salad
ice cream
burgers

fish   pork
meatballs
cheese
peanut butter
soup

.... and ....

.... and ....

.... and ....

.... and ....

.... and ....

.... and ....

.... and ....

.... and ....

.... and ....

.... and ....

.... and ....

.... and ....

Chew on This!

Page Count

You started reading your book on page 15. You read through page 30. How many pages did you read?

Cave Code

Someone wrote a secret message on a cave wall in glow-in-the-dark chalk. Can you find the message amid all these letters?

```
F G H G I F O T Z Y X A B L M N P Y
C I U Y O U H F M S F I N D P A A B
T H I S G V T V W X X Y Z S D R F C
L L T D Z A B C E M E S S A G E F I
J K V N E F G E F E C D R P W I L L
V W E Y O U X E N L K J U I O P Q K
Q W E R O G H D J P L E A S E T I G
Y I M X B D E D T U R N J T T Y O P
A Q I Y L O N H T S J O P Q U G R I
T Y T H E U C F O Q U L I G H T S R
K F I K L J K L Q I T S C A D A R K
D R J K L G P Q I N I O I H E R E I
V C T H A N K D I U I H Y Y O U S I
```

Hint: The only words you'll find are the ones in the message!

114

O Brother!

**At each step down the pyramid, add a letter,
then rearrange the letters to solve the definition.**

O

— — You might say this when
      you're surprised.

— — — Lying in the sun can make
        you feel this way.

— — — — You can have this one or
          that one but not _____.

— — — — — — Another name for soup

— — — — — — — Eeyore's favorite saying is
                "Oh, _____."

B R O T H E R

States of Excitement

Sally was so excited about her family vacation that she mixed up the names of the places she'd visited. Can you rearrange the letters to figure out which states Sally went to?

Sally went to:

1. ham icing

2. eel award

3. vet norm

4. old fair

5. bank ears

6. a mine

7. wins coins

8. ran madly

Bye-Bye!

Say so long to your final word search. Listed words go up, down, backward, forward, and diagonally.

```
A  L  A  T  E  R  G  A  T  O  R  K
R  U  D  E  Y  B  E  Y  B  U  A  Y
R  A  R  C  H  E  E  F  S  T  S  E
I  E  D  E  S  E  N  A  H  A  J  R
V  Y  I  P  V  N  O  R  E  T  E  R
E  B  Y  I  T  O  E  T  J  A  H  A
D  D  E  D  R  A  I  I  U  L  A  D
E  O  B  E  A  E  L  R  Z  C  O  I
R  O  Y  K  K  O  J  T  O  T  G  O
C  G  U  A  S  J  G  N  O  L  O  S
I  Y  T  T  O  I  R  E  E  H  C  T
B  E  F  A  R  E  W  E  L  L  A  F
```

ADIOS (Spanish)	**GOODBYE**
ARRIVEDERCI (Italian)	**JAHANE** (Japanese)
AU REVOIR (French)	**LATER GATOR**
BYE BYE	**SO LONG**
CHEERIO (British)	**TAKE IT EASY**
	TA TA (British)
FAREWELL	**TOT ZIENS** (Dutch)

Answers

page 6

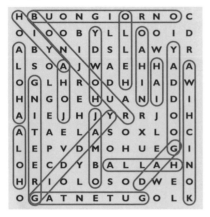

page 7
porcupine/armadillo, chipmunk/squirrel, chimpanzee/kangaroo, woodchuck/anteater, hippopotamus/rhinoceros, reindeer/antelope, elephant/giraffe

page 8–9
Olive opens Oscar's oranges.

Nice, neat narrow noodles never need nuts.

Alive, Alice amuses acorns again. Alone, Abe applauds armadillos.

Black bears bluster. Bold beagles bark. Brave, brash bumblebees bother boisterous boys.

Four flawless flying fairies fetch frail, frightful fallen fowl.

Candy's crazed cat craves cold, chuggable cream.

Danger, dear Dad! Driver Dan drags dinner down drains!

page 9 Chew on This! You walked backward!

page 10
1. black 2. purple 3. brown 4. orange 5. violet 6. scarlet 7. aquamarine 8. lavender

page 11

four steps	five steps
dog	dog
hog	dig
hot	pig
hat	pit
cat	pat
	cat

page 12

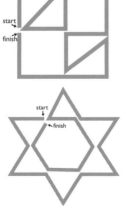

page 13

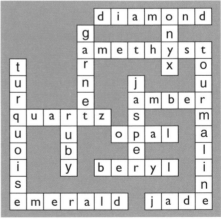

page 14   It All Adds Up: The numbers are in order of how many letters there are in their names. And then, where there are the same number of letters, they are in numerical order. So, 1, 2, 6, 10, 4, 5, 9, 3, 7, 8, 11, 12. What a Funny Way to Count: The numbers are in alphabetical order. So, 80, 50, 40, 90, 70, 60, 10, 30, 20.

page 15 What's black and white and found at the north pole? A lost zebra. What's found in Australia and comes back to you when you throw it? A mad kangaroo.

page 16–17 1. ACROBAT 2. COPYCAT 3. DANDELION 4. OVERBEARING 5. COWARD 6. BILLION 7. CATAPULT 8. KARATE 9. VACATION 10. MEDALLION 11. PIRATE 12. BATHROOM 13. CRATER 14. SCRATCH 15. SCOWL 16. MILLION
The six animals are: bat, bear, cat, cow, lion, rat.

page 17 Chew on This! 19 (17 wheels and 2 steering wheels!)

page 18 What's for lunch today?; leftover pizza; alphabet soup; scrambled eggs with catsup

page 19 What's for dessert?; pumpkin pie; raisin bread; brownies; banana split; lemon pie

page 20 Caitlin—pure; Calista—beautiful; Cara—friend; Casey—brave; Cassidy—clever; Celeste—heavenly; Cerise—cherry red; Colette—victorious; Corazon—heart

page 21

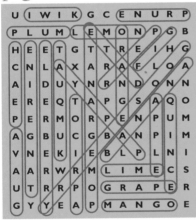

page 22
bobcat, copycat, tomcat, wildcat

flypaper, newspaper, sandpaper, wallpaper

barnyard, courtyard, farmyard, graveyard, shipyard

catfish, goldfish, jellyfish, shellfish, swordfish

billboard, cupboard, dashboard, keyboard, overboard, surfboard

page 23 1. Be home at six for dinner. 2. Your grandma's coming to visit. 3. It's your turn to do the dishes. 4. Will you babysit your brother and sister? 5. Get your homework done before you can play. 6. Good job, dear! You got all A's!

page 24–25 Summer: BACKYARD, LEAPFROG, LAUGHING, THIRSTY, BACKBENDS, LEMONADE Describe It: WONDERFUL, INCREDIBLE, TERRIFYING, SPECTACULAR Oops!: AMBULANCE, BUTTERFINGERS, STUMBLE, ACCIDENT

page 25 Chew on This! The misspelled word is "mispelled"!

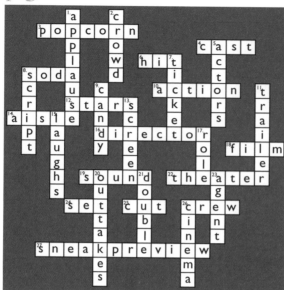

Pick-Up Sticks:

A Giant Ant and a Miniature Whale (Oh Yeah, and a Horse): The whale weighed 500 pounds; the horse, 1,000 pounds; the ant, 2,000 pounds.

page 29 *The Lion King, E.T.—The Extra-Terrestrial, The Wizard of Oz, The Parent Trap, Willy Wonka and the Chocolate Factory, It's a Wonderful Life, Mouse Hunt, Chicken Run, Swiss Family Robinson, Toy Story*

page 30–31 1. vet/jet 2. band/hand 3. kid/lid 4. men/pen 5. fool/pool 6. fan/can 7. jockey/hockey 8. guy/fly 9. banker/tanker 10. groom/broom

page 32 THE LITTLE MERMAID, HANSEL AND GRETEL, SNOW WHITE AND THE SEVEN DWARFS, RUMPELSTILTSKIN, RED RIDING HOOD

page 33 We found **79** possible answers. Did you find more? AID, AIR, AIRY, APE, APIARY, ARID, ART, BAD, BAR, BAY, BID, BIRTH, DAB, DAIRY, DART, DAY, DIAPER, DIARY, DIP, DIPPER, DIRT, DIRTY, EAR, EARTH, EARTHY, HAIR, HAIRY, HAPPY, HARP, HARPER, HAVE, HID, HIP, HOOT, HOT, HYPE, HYPER, OAR, PAID, PAIR, PART, PARTY, PAVE, PAVER, PEA, PEAR, PHOTO, PRAY, PREPAID, PRY, RABID, RAID, RAP, RAPID, RAY, REAP, REPAID, REPAIR, RIB, RID, RIP, RIPE, RIPER, THY, TOAD, TOO, TOOT, TOOTH, TOOTHY, TOT, TOY, TRAP, TRAPPER, TRAY, TRIP, TRY, TYPE, VARY, VERY

page 34 cook I educated, cobweb ready, Tabasco neatly, earmuff in, tapioca ketchup, tomato asteroid, steamroller, piece, firecrackers, amoeba gelatin, popcorn breadfruit, return overjoyed, dough nutty

page 35 RSSH is Rain, Snow, Sleet, Hail; WSSF is Winter, Spring, Summer, Fall; ROYGBIV is Red, Orange, Yellow, Green, Blue, Indigo, Violet; JFMAMJJASOND is January, February, March, April, May, June, July, August, September, October, November, December;

page 35(cont.) MVEMJSUNP is Mercury, Venus, Earth, Mars, Jupiter, Saturn, Uranus, Neptune, Pluto; DDPVCCDB is Dasher, Dancer, Prancer, Vixen, Comet, Cupid, Donner, Blitzen

page 36

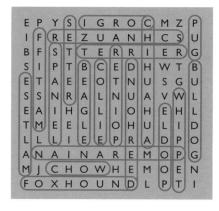

page 37

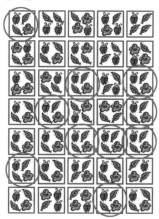

page 38 NO! NO! NO! OREGANO, CASINO, DOMINO, RHINO, KIMONO, PALOMINO, VOLCANO, PIANO; HA! HA! HA! ALOHA, MARTHA, OMAHA

page 39 scar + let = scarlet, drag + on = dragon, pump + kin = pumpkin

page 40–41 1. boat/goat 2. hat/rat 3. log/dog 4. house/mouse 5. bat/cat 6. dish/fish 7. lawn/fawn 8. wizard/lizard

page 41 **Chew on This!** You were standing on the first step.

page 42

page 43 jungle; bananas; swinging; trees

page 45 1. *Sarah, Plain and Tall* 2. *Missing May* 3. *Bud, Not Buddy* 4. *The Westing Game* 5. *From the Mixed-Up Files of Mrs. Basil E. Frankweiler* 6. *Out of the Dust*

page 46–47 corn, oats = cartoons; alone, claw = allowance; done, meal = lemonade; Hansel, pet = elephants

page 48 There are several ways to do this. Here's one:

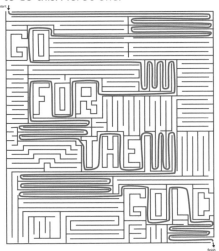

page 49 There are many ways to do this. Here's one:

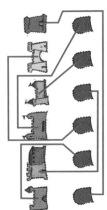

page 50

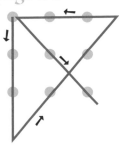

page 50 Chew on This!
HELP I'M TRAPPED INSIDE THIS MIRROR

page 52

			h							
c	l	o	u	d	b	u	r	s	t	
y			r							d
c		f	r	o	s	t		b		r
l			i			h	a	i	l	i
o			c			u		l		z
n			a			n		z		z
e			n			d		z		l
	b	r	e	e	z	e		g	a	l	e
		a				r		r		
		i						d		
m	o	n	s	o	o	n				

page 53 On the Right Hand: Your friend's right elbow
SOOZ OIHO: SIX MINNOWS NOW SWIM IN OHIO ZOOS

page 54

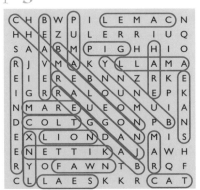

page 55

A
MA
ARM
MARE
CREAM
CAMERA
AMERICA
AMERICAN

page 56 We found 88 possible answers. Did you find more? ABLE, AMBLE, AND, BALD, BAN, BAND, BANDIT, BAR, BARS, BED, BEE, BEET, BET, BID, BIN, BIND, BIT, BITE, BLED, BRAMBLE, BRAN, BRAND, BUMBLEBEE, BUS, BUT, DIET, DIN, EDIBLE, EDIT, EEL, EMBEZZLE, EMBEZZLED, EMU, EMUS, FABLE, FAME, FAN, FAR, FLAB, FLAME, FLIED, FLIT, FLITTED, FLU, FRAME, FUR, FURS, IDLE, LABEL, LABELED, LAMB, LAND, LED, LIBEL, LID, LIE, LIT, MALT, MALTED, MAN, MANDIBLE, MAR, MARS, NAB, NAME, RAFT, RAM, RAMBLE, RAMBLED, RAMS, RAN, RUB, SABLE, SALT, SALTED, SAME, SAND, SUE, SUM, TIDE, TIE, TIED, TILT, TILTED, TIN, TUB, TURF, TURFS

page 57 Clover—Good Luck; Daisy—Innocent; Dandelion—Faithful; Forget-Me-Not—True Love; Iris—Friendship; Pansy—Thoughtful; Red Rose—Love; Sunflower—Proud; Violet—Modest

page 58

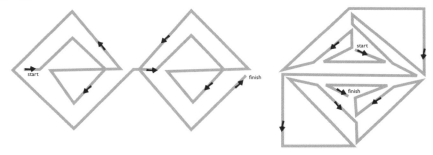

page 59 Pig Latin: **Sage:** What would you do if you saw a blue elephant? **Hope:** I would cheer it up! **Ong:** **Hope:** Why do you think dolphins love to play in salt water? **Sage:** Because pepper water makes them sneeze!

page 60 1. Move the coins on the right side to the left side. 2. Put another sheet of paper on top of the coins. Pick up the paper/coin sandwich, holding the coins carefully in place. Turn the sandwich over, set it on the table, and remove the top piece of paper. Voilà!

page 61 Here's one way:

page 63

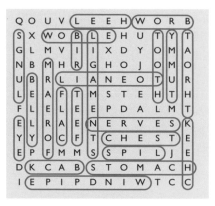

page 66
1. SAD 2. FOLK
3. GNAT 4. SLEEP 5. APE 6. JOLLY

page 67 Four Minus Four Equals . . . Eight?

Cut off the four corners and leave eight sides.

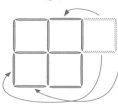

Square It Away 30

page 64–65

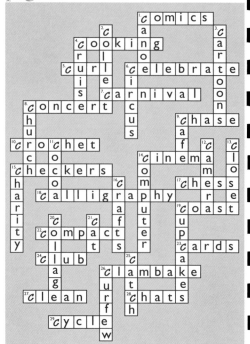

page 68–69
sweet and sour; night and day; horse and buggy; hide and seek; song and dance; pins and needles; cat and mouse; fire and ice; cup and saucer; stars and stripes; table and chairs

page 69 Chew on This! Her grandma!

page 70-71 1. 8 little squares and 2 big squares

2.

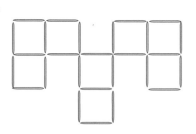

3.

page 71 Chew on This! 1 + 1 + 2 = 4

page 72

page 73 DING DING DING
WEDDING, BUILDING, PUDDING, READING, KIDDING, SPEEDING; SO SO SO PESO, CALYPSO, PICASSO, ALSO

page 74
There are many ways to do this. Here's one:

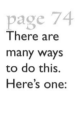

page 76

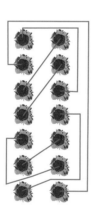

page 77

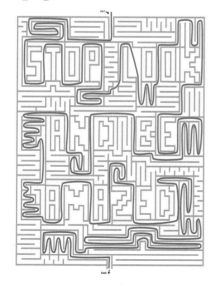

page 78
1. two 2. Two 3. one, one 4. Two, three 5. two 6. two 7. Two, one 8. three 9. one, one 10. three

page 79
OTTFFSSENTET is One, Two, Three, Four, Five, Six, Seven, Eight, Nine, Ten, Eleven, Twelve; DRMFSLTD is Do, Re, Mi, Fa, So, La, Ti, Do; RGYBO is Red, Green, Yellow, Blue, Orange; CVS is Chocolate, Vanilla, Strawberry; PNDQ is Pennies, Nickels, Dimes, Quarters

page 80
1. peach 2. cream 3. magenta 4. silver 5. lilac 6. beige 7. tangerine 8. turquoise

page 81 We found **97** possible answers. Did you find more? AIL, AND, CHIN, CHINA, CHINS, CHOOSE, CHOSE, CHOSEN, CINEMA, CLAM, CLAMS, CLASH, DEER, DEN, DENIAL, DONE, DOSE, DOUSE, EMU, EMUS, END, ENDS, HEM, HERE, HINDER, HIS, HIT, HOOD, HOSE, HOUSE, HUM, HUMAN, HUMANE, HUT, ISLAND, ISLANDS, LAND, LASH, LATIN, LINE, LINES, MAIL, MAIN, MAINE, MANE, MASH, MAT, MATINEE, MEN, MEND, MERMEN, MUSH, MUTINEER, MUTINOUS, NAIL, NAILS, NAME, NOSE, ODE, ONE, RED, REED, REMAIN, REMAINDER, SAIL, SAILS, SALTINES, SAME, SAND, SATIN, SCHOONER, SEE, SEEM, SEND, SHE, SHEER, SHIN, SHINE, SHONE, SHUT, SIT, SLAM, SMASH, SNAIL, SON, SOON, SOONER, SUMMER, TAIL, TAME, TAN, TIN, TINDER, USE, USED, USER, USHER

page 82 There are 83 Q's.

page 83 There are 52 cones.

page 84 ELEMENTARY, BLACKBOARD, QUARTERBACK, ALPHABETICAL

page 85 Pearl is a Siberian husky, Prince is a Chihuahua, Prancer is a collie, and Pepper is a Great Dane. Prancer won the blue ribbon.

page 86–87 Five-foot Fannie fights firey flames from floating ferries. Teddy teased the twins till they tired. Thanks, Teddy!
Grim, grave ghosts grasp Grace's glittering, glistening gown. Gail gasps, "Gross!"
Rowena rarely records rap. Roxie regularly replays rock.
Elena eats eggplant every evening.
Mad Mabel made meek Mandy march many miles. "March, Mandy, march," muttered Mabel. Mandy merely moaned.

page 88–89

page 90–91

1. meal/seal
2. cloth/sloth
3. pear/bear
4. road/toad
5. fog/hog
6. mitten/kitten
7. wig/pig
8. jam/ram

page 91 **Chew on This!** The cattle ranchers were women riding in a truck.

page 92 Just One Word: You can rearrange the letters to spell "just one word." Wrong, Wrong, Wrong: pearagraph, fined, and the statement that there are three mistakes, because there are only two. (Of course, then you could say that yes, there are three mistakes, so the statement that there are three mistakes is correct, which would make it not a mistake, which means there are only two mistakes, which means that the statement is no longer correct, which means that . . . if you think about this long enough, your head will explode.)

A Longer Word: a longer word than you wrote

page 93 daylight, flashlight, floodlight, headlight, moonlight, searchlight, skylight, spotlight, sunlight; handbook, matchbook, textbook, workbook, yearbook; eyeball, football, snowball, softball

page 94 Balls, sand castles, seashells, sunscreen, net, tide pool, lagoons, sand dollar, radio, outside

page 95 Start off hand stand out side kick box car top dog leg room service station wagon train track suit case study hall way side dish water color blind date book store front end

page 96 1. *The View from Saturday* 2. *Julie of the Wolves* 3. *Walk Two Moons* 4. *Holes* 5. *Number the Stars* 6. *The Giver* 7. *Dear Mr. Henshaw*

page 97 Elton John was Reginald Kenneth Dwight, Cher was Cherilyn Sarkesian, Tom Cruise was Thomas C. Mapother, Meg Ryan was Margaret Hyra, Whoopi Goldberg was Caryn Johnson, Enya was Eithne Ni Bhraonain, Babyface was Kenneth Brian Edmonds, Sting was Gordon Sumner, Sinbad was David Adkins

page 98–99 yell + ow = yellow; tan + go = tango; ad + dress = address; car + pet = carpet; her + ring = herring; pup + pet = puppet; sea + son = season; pop + corn = popcorn

page 100–101 dry, habit = birthday; grader, month = grandmother; peel, solver = sleepover

page 101 **Chew on This!** One. The person sitting has two legs, the chair has four legs, and the table has four legs.

page 102

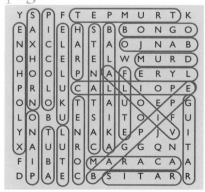

page 103 Morgan likes James; Jasmine likes Jason; Karina likes Logan; Lindsey likes Lancaster

page 104–105 1. REBATE 2. DEBATE 3. DEDICATE 4. BEARD 5. PIGMENT 6. WOMBAT 7. GRATE 8. LOCATE 9. PIGEON 10. SPIGOT, 11. NARRATE 12. DELICATE 13. MARATHON 14. UNBEARABLE
The five animals are: rat, bat, cat, bear, pig.

page 106 orangutan/gorilla; dolphin/octopus; eagle/parrot; leopard/panther; hedgehog/badger; penguin/walrus

page 107

(The number eight!) (The roman numeral six)

page 108 1. straight A's 2. I want to be in the movies. 3. bacon and eggs 4. a balanced meal 5. a sleepover this weekend

page 109 BEAUTY AND THE BEAST, THE UGLY DUCKLING, THE PRINCESS AND THE PEA, JACK AND THE BEANSTALK

page 110

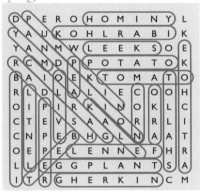

page 111 1. daughter/water 2. wife/knife 3. fairy/dairy 4. cast/mast 5. crook/brook 6. witch/ditch

page 112–113 spaghetti and meatballs; bacon and eggs; burgers and fries; fish and chips; soup and salad; cake and ice cream; peanut butter and jelly; macaroni and cheese; pork and beans; milk and cookies; meat and potatoes; porkchops and applesauce

page 113 Chew on This! 16

page 114 IF YOU FIND THIS MESSAGE, WILL YOU PLEASE TURN ON THE LIGHTS? IT'S DARK IN HERE. THANK YOU.

page 115

O
O H
H O T
B O T H
B R O T H
B O T H E R
B R O T H E R

page 116 1. Michigan 2. Delaware 3. Vermont 4. Florida 5. Nebraska 6. Maine 7. Wisconsin 8. Maryland

page 117

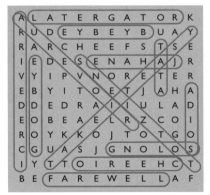

Try it risk-free!

American Girl magazine is especially for girls 8 and up. Send for your preview issue today! Mail this card to receive a risk-free preview issue and start your one-year subscription. For just $22.95, you'll receive 6 bimonthly issues in all! If you don't love it right away, just write "cancel" on the invoice and return it to us. The preview issue is yours to keep, free!

Send bill to: (please print)

_____
Adult's name

_____
Address

_____
City   State   Zip

_____
Adult's signature

Send magazine to: (please print)

_____
Girl's name   Birth date *(optional)*

_____
Address

_____
City   State   Zip

Guarantee: You may cancel at any time for a full refund. Allow 4–6 weeks for first issue. Non-U.S. subscriptions $29 U.S., prepaid only.
© 2004 American Girl, LLC.   K43AGL

Free catalogue!

Welcome to a world that's all yours—because it's filled with the things girls love! Beautiful dolls that capture your heart. Books that send your imagination soaring. And games and pastimes that make being a girl great!

For your free American Girl® catalogue, return this postcard, call 1-800-845-0005, or visit our Web site at americangirl.com.

Send me a catalogue:

_____/____/____
Name   Girl's birth date

_____
Address

_____
City   State   Zip

_____
E-mail *(Fill in to receive order information, updates, and Web-exclusive offers.)*

(_____)_____
Phone   ❑ Home ❑ Work

Send my friend a catalogue:

_____
Name

_____
Address

_____
City   State   Zip

                                          12591i

_____
Parent's signature   12583i